SAMURAI

JAPAN'S NOBLE
SERVANT-WARRIORS

By Blake Hoena
Illustrated by János Orbán

Consultant:
Tim Solie
Adjunct Professor of History
Minnesota State University, Mankato
Mankato, Minnesota

CAPSTONE PRESS
a capstone imprint

Graphic Library is published by Capstone Press,
1710 Roe Crest Drive, North Mankato, Minnesota 56003
www.mycapstone.com

Library of Congress Cataloging-in-Publication data
Names: Hoena, B. A., author. | Orbán, János, illustrator.
Title: Samurai : Japan's noble servant-warriors / by Blake Hoena ; illustrated by János Orbán.
 Other titles: Japan's noble servant-warriors
Description: North Mankato, Minnesota : Capstone Press, [2019] | Series: Graphic library.
 Graphic history: warriors | Includes bibliographical references and index. | Audience:
 Grades 4–6. | Audience: Ages 8–12.
Identifiers: LCCN 2018031870 (print) | LCCN 2018034461 (ebook) | ISBN 9781543555127
 (eBook PDF) | ISBN 9781543555042 (library binding) | ISBN 9781543559309 (paperback)
Subjects: LCSH: Samurai—Juvenile literature. | Graphic novels—Juvenile literature.
Classification: LCC DS827.S3 (ebook) | LCC DS827.S3 H666 2019 (print) |
 DDC 952/.025—dc23
LC record available at https://lccn.loc.gov/2018031870

Summary: In graphic novel format, tells several tales of famous samurai while exploring the
history, armor, weapons, and battles of these noble warriors from feudal Japan.

EDITOR
Aaron J. Sautter

ART DIRECTOR
Nathan Gassman

DESIGNER
Ted Williams

MEDIA RESEARCHER
Jo Miller

PRODUCTION SPECIALIST
Kathy McColley

Design Elements: Shutterstock: michelaubryphoto, Reinhold Leitner

Printed and bound in the United States of America.
PA48

TABLE OF CONTENTS

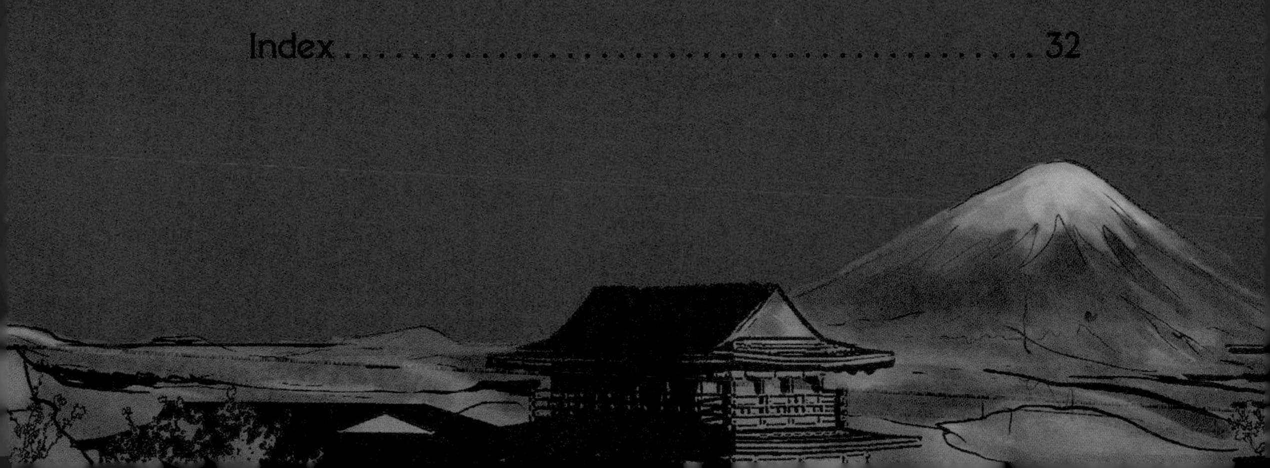

THOSE WHO SERVE

The samurai began as professional warriors, working for rich land owners. They also served as guards for nobles and the emperor. The word *samurai* translates to "those who served." The samurai grew in importance during Japan's Heian Period (AD 794–1185). This era was named after Heian-kyō, the modern-day city of Kyōto. It was the imperial capital of Japan and the seat of central government.

Today, we will defeat the Taira and the city will be ours.

Over time, the influence of the samurai grew. Two families, the Taira and Minamoto clans, rose to power in Japan. They fought for control of the government.

Hurry! We must ride out to defend the city!

Attack!

FWIP! THUMP!

THWIP! THUMP!

Minamoto Yoritomo led the Minamoto clan during the Genpei War (1180–1185).

YAAAA!

AAIIEEE!

RAARR!

The Minamoto clan drove the Taira out of Kyōto in 1183.

In 1192 Minamoto Yoritomo declared himself to be *shōgun*, Japan's military leader. For the next 700 years, samurai clans fought to control Japan and its feudal system of government. Over the years, the achievements of several samurai warriors helped seal their place in history.

TRAINING A MIGHTY WARRIOR

As the samurai's influence grew, so did their status in Japanese society. They went from being professional soldiers to land-owning nobles. The most powerful of these lords were called *daimyos*.

Hold your *bokuto* out in front of you, with both hands, like you would a *katana*.

To become a samurai, a person usually had to be born into a samurai family. Miyamoto Musashi's father was Shinmen Munisai, a skilled samurai swordsman.

Starting at a young age, Musashi's father began teaching him to fight with a bokuto, or wooden sword. He learned quickly.

CLACK!

Good!

Samurai also learned archery using a bow called a *yumi*.

Draw the string back with your thumb. Calm your breath as you aim, and then release.

THUNK!

6

Samurai learned many other skills during their training. After his father died, Musashi went to study with his uncle, a Buddhist monk. He learned to read and write. He studied poetry and became a skilled painter.

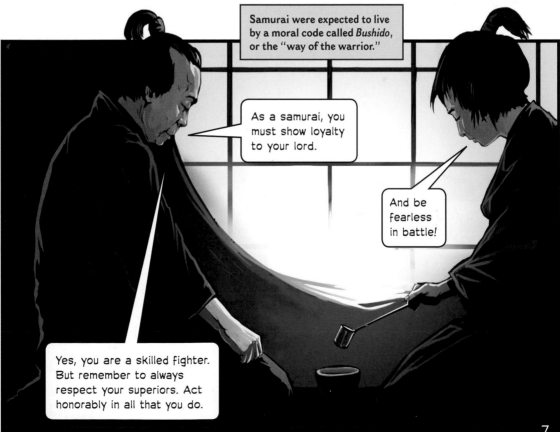

Samurai were expected to live by a moral code called *Bushido*, or the "way of the warrior."

As a samurai, you must show loyalty to your lord.

And be fearless in battle!

Yes, you are a skilled fighter. But remember to always respect your superiors. Act honorably in all that you do.

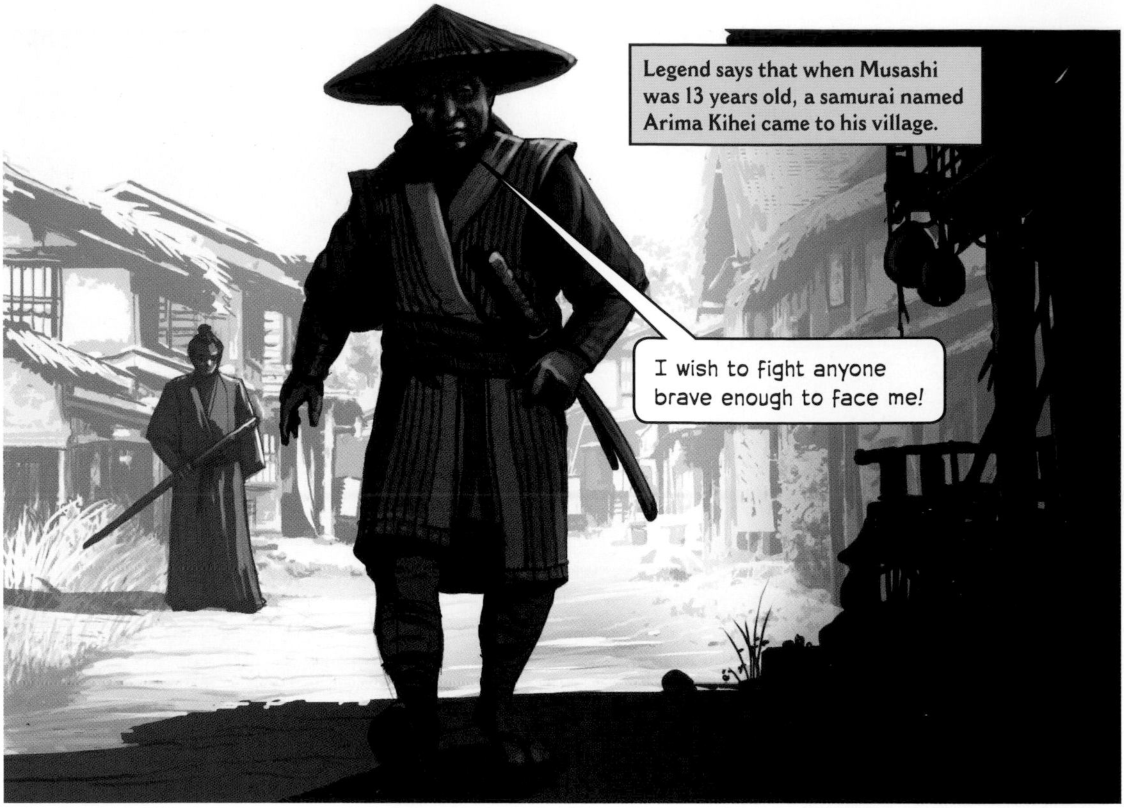
Legend says that when Musashi was 13 years old, a samurai named Arima Kihei came to his village.
I wish to fight anyone brave enough to face me!

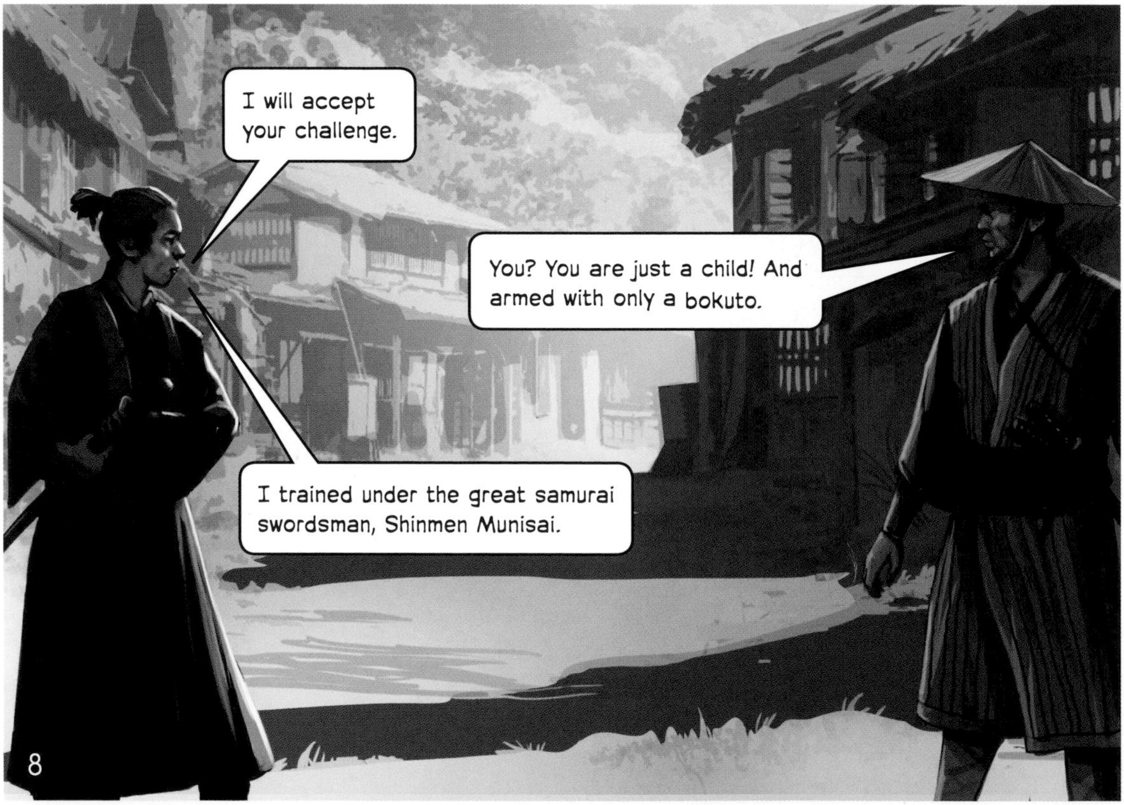
I will accept your challenge.
You? You are just a child! And armed with only a bokuto.
I trained under the great samurai swordsman, Shinmen Munisai.

Shortly after the fight began, Arima Kihei learned his mistake.

WOOSH!

THUMP!

YAAHH!

CRUNCH!

Underestimating Musashi's skill cost the prideful samurai his life.

With his initial training complete, Musashi left his uncle and his village. He wished to learn more and improve his sword fighting skills.

Don't forget the way of the warrior, my nephew.

Yes, Uncle. I will always remember.

For much of his life, Musashi lived as a *ronin*, or masterless samurai. He wandered the country, challenging the best swordsmen in Japan.

Ganryu Island is up ahead. Are you sure that a sword carved from an oar will be good enough to win?

Yes. This wooden sword is all I need to defeat Kojirō.

On April 13, 1612, Musashi agreed to fight Sasaki Kojirō, a skilled fighter who used a long, two-handed sword.

Musashi purposely arrived late to the duel. He knew that it would irritate Kojirō.

You are hours late. How disrespectful!

I was thinking you were too much of a coward to face me.

I am here now, and ready.

Annoyed by Musashi's disrespect, Kojirō lost his focus. He swung his sword angrily at his opponent, but he was no match for Musashi's skill.

HYAAH!

FFWISH!

Musashi took advantage of his opponent's anger. He quickly struck Kojirō down with his crude wooden sword.

Legends say that Miyamoto Musashi fought in 60 duels, and won all of them. He became one of the greatest swordsmen in samurai history. Later in life, Miyamoto wrote about his training and duels in *Go Rin No Sho*, or *The Book of Five Rings*. The book also described his thoughts and strategies on how to win any conflict.

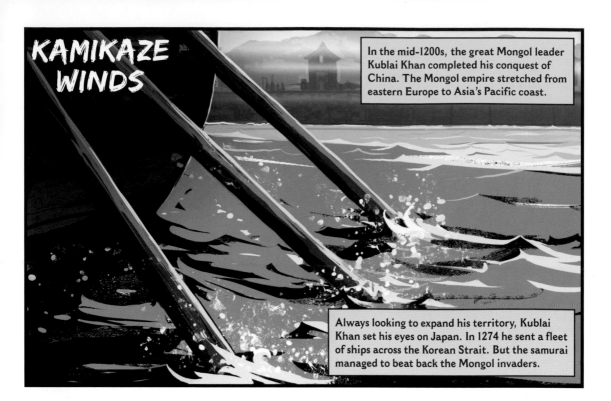

KAMIKAZE WINDS

In the mid-1200s, the great Mongol leader Kublai Khan completed his conquest of China. The Mongol empire stretched from eastern Europe to Asia's Pacific coast.

Always looking to expand his territory, Kublai Khan set his eyes on Japan. In 1274 he sent a fleet of ships across the Korean Strait. But the samurai managed to beat back the Mongol invaders.

Seven years later, the Mongols launched a second invasion. But the Japanese warriors were prepared. They built a wall protecting Hakata Bay along Japan's southwestern coast.

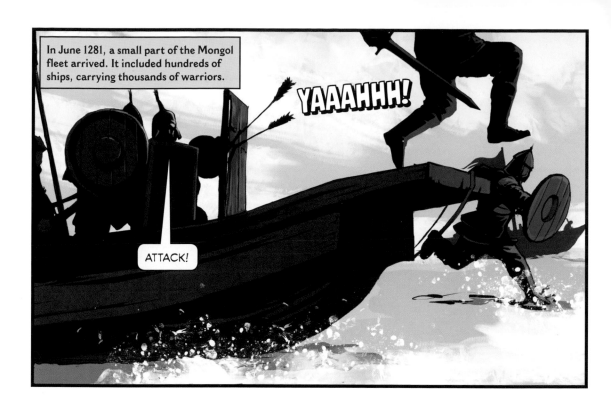

In June 1281, a small part of the Mongol fleet arrived. It included hundreds of ships, carrying thousands of warriors.

YAAAHHH!

ATTACK!

As the Mongol invaders charged up the beach, the samurai let loose with their deadliest weapons.

FWIP!

THUNK!

AAGGH!

THWIP!

THWIP!

THUNK!

UUHHG!

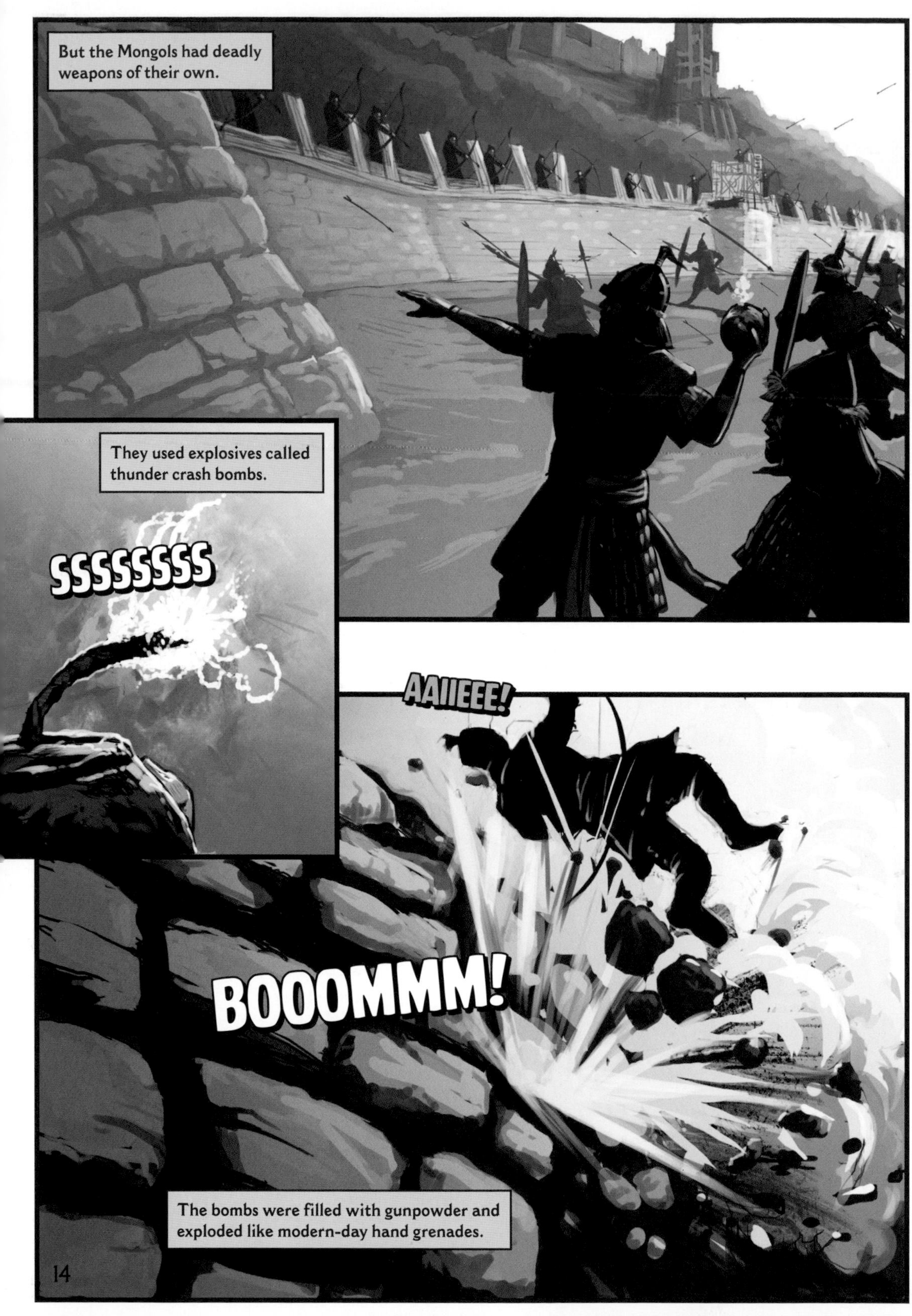
But the Mongols had deadly weapons of their own.
They used explosives called thunder crash bombs.
SSSSSSSS
AAIIEEE!
BOOOMMM!
The bombs were filled with gunpowder and exploded like modern-day hand grenades.

During the day, the samurai and Mongol warriors battled on the beach. But at night, the samurai snuck out to sea.

THUNK!

FWOOSSH!

They set fire to many of the Mongol ships.

After nearly two months of fighting, the battle was at a stalemate. Neither side could defeat the other.

Then in August 1281, the main Mongol fleet arrived. Thousands of ships carried tens of thousands of warriors.

The samurai were impossibly outnumbered. But just days after the fleet arrived, a typhoon blew into the bay.

The Japanese called the storm a *kamikaze*, or "divine wind." They believed it was sent by the gods to protect their island.

The typhoon destroyed the Mongol fleet. Most of the ships sank, and thousands of Mongol warriors drowned.

The Mongols who swam to shore were quickly killed by the samurai. After the defeat at Hakata Bay, Kublai Khan gave up his hopes of conquering Japan.

The gods have favored us.

Yes, but we must always be ready to defend our land.

The samurai protected Japan from invaders and foreigners for hundreds of years. They didn't want people from the outside world corrupting their way of life.

THE MASTER STRATEGIST

In 1331 Kusunoki Masashige was a modest landowner. But during the Genkō War (1331–1333), Masashige's strategic leadership in battle would make him famous.

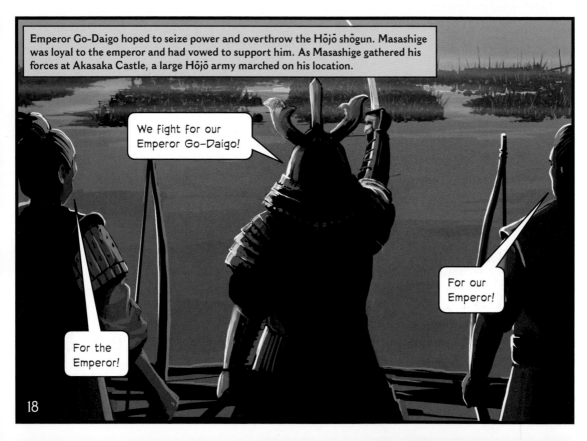

Emperor Go-Daigo hoped to seize power and overthrow the Hōjō shōgun. Masashige was loyal to the emperor and had vowed to support him. As Masashige gathered his forces at Akasaka Castle, a large Hōjō army marched on his location.

THWIP! THWIP! THWIP! THWIP!

When the enemy attacked, Masashige bravely led the defense on the castle walls.

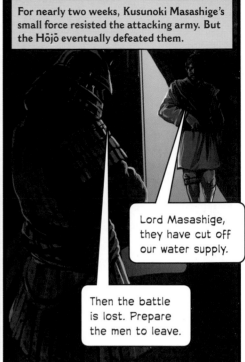

For nearly two weeks, Kusunoki Masashige's small force resisted the attacking army. But the Hōjō eventually defeated them.

Lord Masashige, they have cut off our water supply.

Then the battle is lost. Prepare the men to leave.

Masashige set fire to the castle to cover their escape.

The Hōjō will think we died. It will take them a while to realize we escaped. They won't follow us right away.

Masashige and his men escaped to Mount Kongo. There they built a small fortress called Chihaya Castle to prepare for another attack by the shōgun's forces.

When the Hōjō soldiers attacked, Masashige's men rained down rocks and arrows on them. Thousands of men were killed and injured.

THWIP!

THWIP!

THUNK!

AAAGGH!

When the Hōjō army attacked again, Masashige's forces rolled large logs down the hill at the soldiers. Hundreds more were killed or injured.

AAARRRGH!

RUMMMMBLE!

AAAIIEEEE!

In yet another attempt, the Hōjō built a bridge across a ravine protecting the castle. Masashige's men pumped oil into the ravine and set it on fire, forcing the attackers to flee.

Masashige's heroics gave courage to other samurai. Soon more began to rebel against the shōgun. Emperor Go-Daigo gained control of the government for a brief time.

But a few years after the Emperor's victory, another group of samurai rebelled against him. Once again, Kusunoki Masashige came to the emperor's aid. However, this time the heroic samurai was defeated by the overwhelming forces he faced.

If only I had seven lives to give to my emperor.

Aye, then maybe we could win this battle.

Masashige has become a national hero in Japan. He is admired for the unbending loyalty he showed to his emperor.

THE THREE UNIFIERS

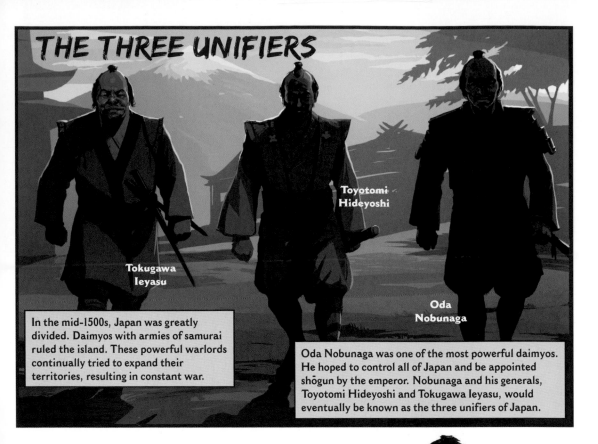

Tokugawa
Ieyasu

Toyotomi
Hideyoshi

Oda
Nobunaga

In the mid-1500s, Japan was greatly divided. Daimyos with armies of samurai ruled the island. These powerful warlords continually tried to expand their territories, resulting in constant war.

Oda Nobunaga was one of the most powerful daimyos. He hoped to control all of Japan and be appointed shōgun by the emperor. Nobunaga and his generals, Toyotomi Hideyoshi and Tokugawa Ieyasu, would eventually be known as the three unifiers of Japan.

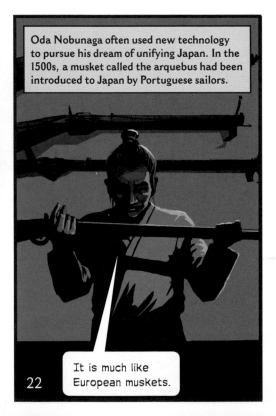

Oda Nobunaga often used new technology to pursue his dream of unifying Japan. In the 1500s, a musket called the arquebus had been introduced to Japan by Portuguese sailors.

It is much like European muskets.

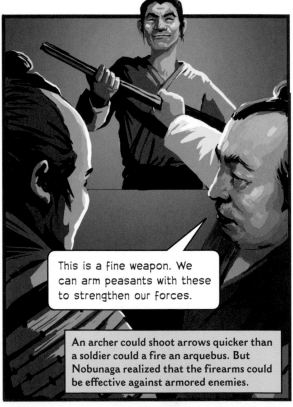

This is a fine weapon. We can arm peasants with these to strengthen our forces.

An archer could shoot arrows quicker than a soldier could a fire an arquebus. But Nobunaga realized that the firearms could be effective against armored enemies.

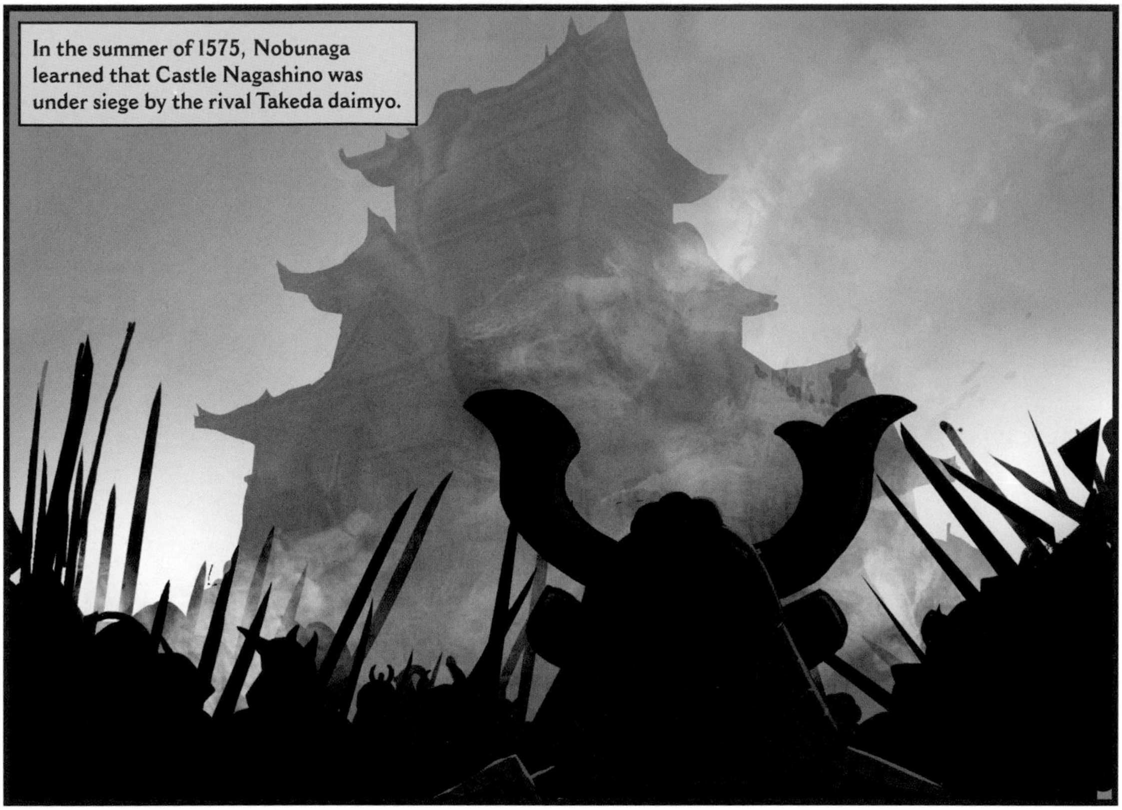
In the summer of 1575, Nobunaga learned that Castle Nagashino was under siege by the rival Takeda daimyo.

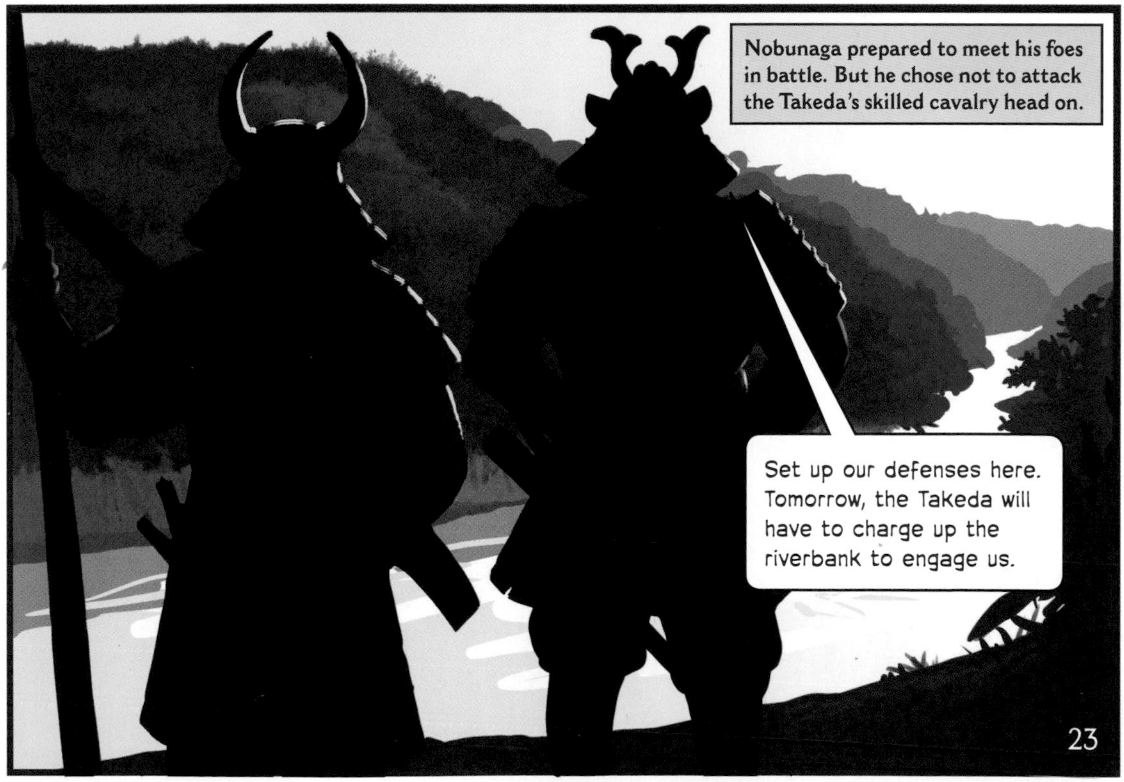
Nobunaga prepared to meet his foes in battle. But he chose not to attack the Takeda's skilled cavalry head on.
Set up our defenses here. Tomorrow, the Takeda will have to charge up the riverbank to engage us.

Nobunaga's army included about 1,000 men armed with arquebus weapons. Some soldiers were shooters and others were loaders. As the shooters aimed and fired, the loaders continually reloaded and prepared the weapons to be fired.

YAAAAAHH!!

Charge!

On the morning of June 28, 1575, the Takeda cavalry charged across the river.

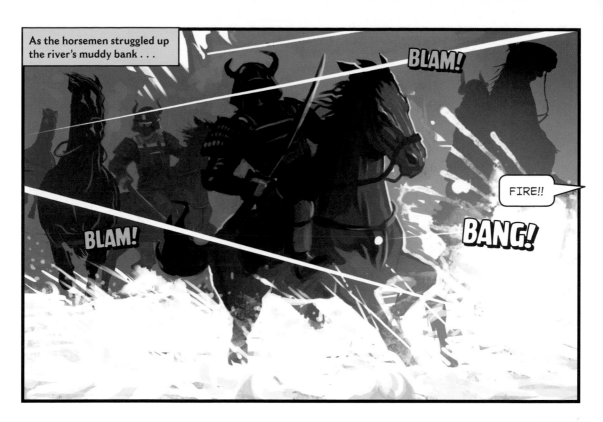

As the horsemen struggled up the river's muddy bank . . .

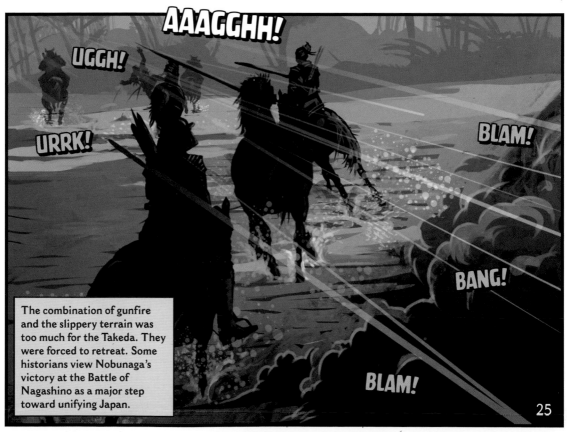

The combination of gunfire and the slippery terrain was too much for the Takeda. They were forced to retreat. Some historians view Nobunaga's victory at the Battle of Nagashino as a major step toward unifying Japan.

Ieyasu, if you support my efforts against the Hōjō, you can rule their lands.

Oda Nobunaga died in 1582. His general Toyotomi Hideyoshi then seized power. Many daimyos loyal to Nobunaga supported Hideyoshi, but others opposed him. He defeated some of them in battle while others, like Tokugawa Ieyasu, had to be convinced to join him.

It's agreed then. I'll join my forces with yours.

By 1590, only the Hōjō clan stood against Hideyoshi. Their stronghold was Castle Odawara.

With our combined forces, we will win this siege. The Hōjō will be forced to surrender.

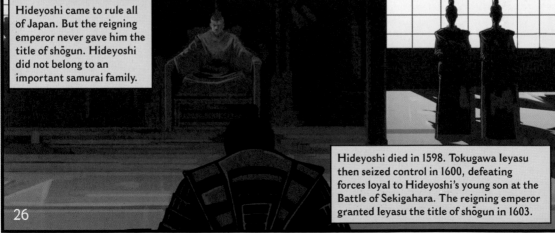

Hideyoshi came to rule all of Japan. But the reigning emperor never gave him the title of shōgun. Hideyoshi did not belong to an important samurai family.

Hideyoshi died in 1598. Tokugawa Ieyasu then seized control in 1600, defeating forces loyal to Hideyoshi's young son at the Battle of Sekigahara. The reigning emperor granted Ieyasu the title of shōgun in 1603.

Ieyasu ushered in the Edo Period (1603–1868), an era ruled by his family. It was also a time of great change in Japanese society. Samurai were feudal lords who mostly ruled farmland. But as more and more people moved to larger cities, such as Tokyo, the samurai began to lose their influence and wealth.

By the mid-1800s Western countries began sending ships to Japan, demanding to trade with the island nation. In the past, the samurai had kept foreign nations out. But the samurai could not match the military forces of countries like the United States. Many Japanese people, including some samurai, saw that changes were needed if Japan was going to remain an independent nation.

Economic and political conflicts led to the Meiji Restoration in 1868. After 700 years, the emperor regained complete control of the government. Soon after, Japan created a national army and the samurai class was abolished. The age of the samurai had come to an end.

MORE ABOUT SAMURAI

1

Hakata Bay—Samurai warriors fought and defeated the second Mongol invasion at the Second Battle of Hakata Bay in 1281.

2

Chihaya Castle—Masashige Kusunoki built Chihaya Castle atop Mount Kongo. Masashige used the mountain's steep sides to help hold off a large army during the Siege of Chihaya in 1333.

3

Castle Nagashino—During the Battle of Nagashino in 1575, Oda Nobunaga's army fired muskets from behind a wooden wall to repel the Takeda cavalry. It is often considered the first "modern" Japanese battle.

4

Osaka Castle—Built in 1583, the Toyotomi clan ruled most of Japan from Osaka Castle until it was overthrown in 1615.

5

Castle Odawara—In 1590 Toyotomi Hideyoshi laid siege to Castle Odawara to defeat the Hōjō clan. The siege lasted for three months before the Hōjō surrendered.

6

Sekigahara—Tokugawa Ieyasu defeated his enemies at the Battle of Sekigahara in 1600. His victory at Sekigahara led to his rule of Japan.

7

Ganryu Island—Miyamoto Musashi and Sasaki Kojirō fought a deadly duel on Ganryu in 1612. Today, monuments to this legendary battle are found on the island.

8

Heian-kyō—Known today as Kyōto, this was the imperial capital of Japan during the reign of the samurai.

9

Tokyo—The modern day capital of Japan.

IMPORTANT LOCATIONS OF FEUDAL JAPAN

Samurai needed to be quick and nimble while fighting in battle. Their armor was constructed with many small parts to keep it flexible. Overlapping scales of hardened leather or metal were tied together with leather or silk lacings. A colored lacquer was then applied to help seal and protect the armor.

Samurai began using steel plate armor in the 1500s. The overlapping plates better protected the samurai against gunfire. The structure of samurai armor influenced the design of modern-day bulletproof vests.

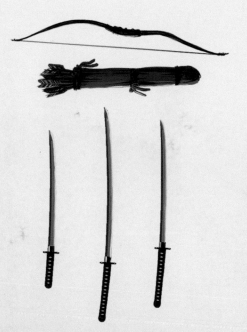

Samurai warriors often used bows and arrows and swords in combat. The sword was a samurai's deadliest weapon. Swords were also a status symbol, and samurai didn't go anywhere without them.

Early samurai swords had straight, double-edged blades made of iron. Over time, a curve was added to the blade. This shape gave the swords better striking power and made them easier to draw, especially on horseback. Master swordsmiths also learned special methods for forging steel swords such as *tachis*, *katanas*, and *wakizashis*. These swords were strong, flexible, and stayed razor-sharp.

GLOSSARY

arquebus (AHR-kwuh-buhs)—a type of long-barreled musket gun used in the 1500s

bokuto (bo-KOO-do)—a wooden practice sword

Bushido (BOO-shee-do)—Japanese code of honor that samurai lived by; the code demands complete loyalty and obedience, and values honor before one's own life

cavalry (KA-vuhl-ree)—soldiers who travel and fight on horseback

clan (KLAN)—a large group of families and related people

daimyo (DY-mee-oh)—a nobleman or samurai lord who owned a great deal of land

era (EER-uh)—a period of history marked by significant historical people or events

feudal system (FYOOD-uhl SIS-tuhm)—a system of government in the Middle Ages in which samurai received land for their military service; common people then worked the land for the samurai

kamikaze (kah-mi-KAH-zee)—Japanese word meaning "divine wind"

noble (NOH-buhl)—a person of high rank or birth

shōgun (SHOH-guhn)—a military general who once ruled Japan

siege (SEEJ)—an attack designed to surround a fort or city to cut it off from supplies or help

typhoon (tie-FOON)—a hurricane that forms in the western Pacific Ocean

READ MORE

Bodden, Valerie. *Samurai.* X-Books: Fighters. Mankato, Minn.: Creative Education. 2018.

Farndon, John. *How to Live Like a Samurai Warrior.* How to Live Like…. Minneapolis: Hungry Tomato, 2016.

Lusted, Marcia Amidon. *Samurai Science: Armor, Weapons, and Battlefield Strategy.* Warrior Science. North Mankato, Minn.: Capstone Press, 2017.

CRITICAL THINKING QUESTIONS

- Most samurai faithfully served and fought for a lord or emperor. But a few samurai lived alone as ronin. They studied swordsmanship and fought in many duels. If you were a samurai, which path would you follow? Would you serve a lord or fight for yourself? Explain your answer.

- Samurai rose to power in Japan at about the same time as medieval knights in Europe. Compare what you know about knights to what you've learned about samurai. How are samurai and medieval knights similar? How are they different?

- Turn to pages 10–11, in which Miyamoto Musashi fights Sasaki Kojirō. Do you feel it is fair that Miyamoto showed up late to the duel? How did this affect Kojirō? Can you think of modern ways in which people might cause an opponent to lose focus, whether in sports or games?

INTERNET SITES

Use Facthound to find Internet sites related to this book.

Visit **www.*facthound*.com**

Just type in 9781543555011 and go.

Check out projects, games and lots more at
www.capstonekids.com

INDEX